AF505181
Would You
Rather Game
Book For Kids
6-12 Years
Old
LOL

GIFT
Claim Your FREE Printable Colored Bookmarks From

https://rebrand.ly/freebookmarks

Hey! Thanks for purchasing this book and hope it helps you on your journey. All feedback on Amazon is appreciated. We have put a lot of effort into this title, so if you are not completely satisfied email us at thechikkupublishing@gmail.com. You're **INVITED** to receive a **Digital copy of 2021 Planner** at www.chikkupublishing.com

Do Check Out Our Store For More Similar Book!

Would You RATHER ...

Jump Across A Fence Or Sit
Still Like A Stone?

Have A Water For 1 Day Or Soda
For The Rest Of Your Life?

Would You RATHER ...

Be Able To Live 1000 Years Old Or Be The Strongest Man Alive?

Have A Moustache Or Have Big Head?

Would You RATHER ...

Not See Red & Green Color That Everyone Can Or Clear The Dustbin Everyday?

Be A Small Zebra or A Dinosaur Sized Zebra?

Would You RATHER ...

Eat Ice Cream With Cherry Topping Or Banana Skin With Pudding?

Drink Water From A Baby Bottle Or Soda From A Water Cooler?

Would You RATHER ...

Have X-ray Eyes
Or Ears That Can Hear Ants Speak?

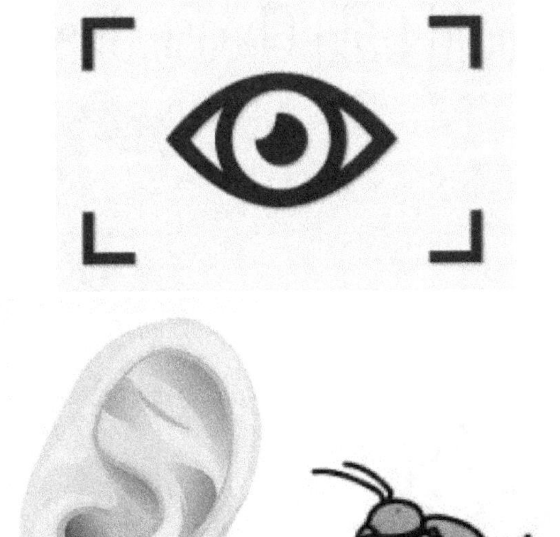

Colored Hair Or Nicely Gelled Hair?

Would You RATHER ...

Sit Down And Dream Or Stand Up And Sing Forever If You Could Only Choose One?

Play With Your Toys Or Read A New Story Book?

Would You RATHER ...

Receive Your Pocket Money
In Pennies Or Dollar Bills ?

Have A Fight In School Or
Street Fight With A Bully?

Would You RATHER ...

Eat Cat Food Or Dog Treats
For Dessert After Each Meal?

Sweat Cotton Candy Or Have
Your Breath Always Smell Like
Salmon Fish?

Would You RATHER ...

Have To Drink Everything From Your Nose Or Eat Everything With Your Feets?

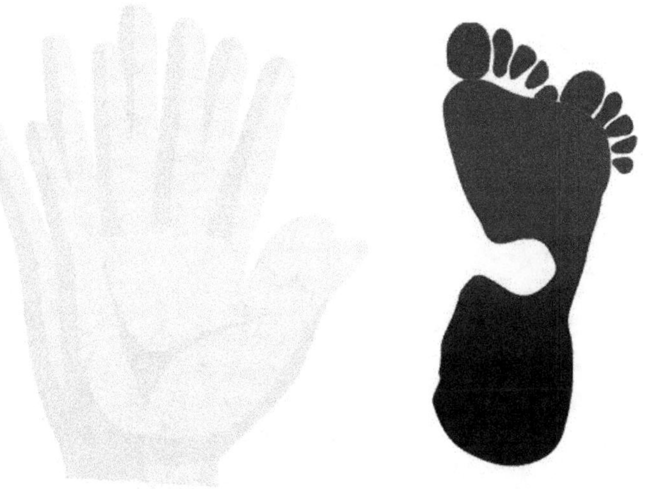

Have 10 Fingers And Toes On One Hand Or 1 Finger On Both Hands?

Would You RATHER ...

Eat However Many Gummy Bears Or French Fries You Wanted?

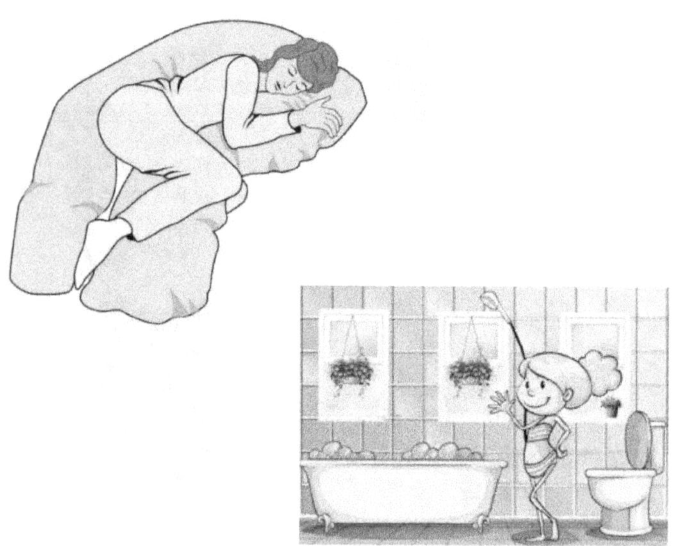

Never Have To Sleep More Than 3 Hours Every Day Or Never Have To Go Shower?

Would You RATHER ...

Have To Sit On A Birthday Cake Or Be Slimed All Over Your Face?

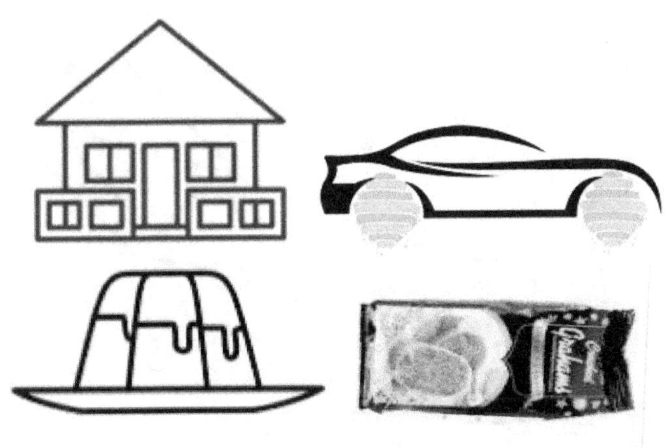

Live In A House That Is Sit On Jelly Or Car Have Wheels Made With Honey Comb?

Would You RATHER ...

Have To Eat Two Ice Cube At A Go Or Sniff One Small Pinch Of Pepper?

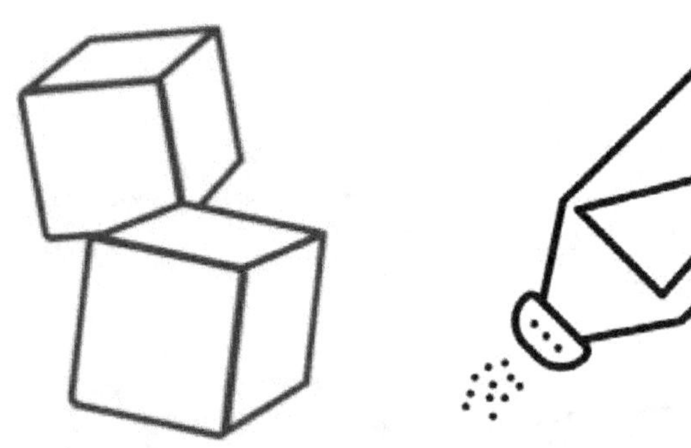

Sound Like A Crow Every Time You Laughed Or Sound Like A Dog Every Time Your Screamed?

Would You RATHER ...

Teleport Into A Toilet
Or Into A Classroom?

Be A Superhero Who Cannot Fly Or
One Who Could Run Super Fast?

Would You RATHER ...

Sleep Whole Day Or Play Video Game
For The Rest Of Your Life?

Have To Use Your Weak Hand To
Brush Teeth Or To Click A Mouse?

Would You RATHER ...

Lose All Of Your Hair
Or Wear Dentures For Life?

Float Every Time You Sleep Or
Sing Every Time You Tried To
Walk?

Would You RATHER ...

Have To Sneeze Paper Every Time You Watch TV Or Have Hiccups Everyday You Play Mobile Games?

Possess The Power To Never Forget Or To Never Get Scolding From Teachers And Parents?

Would You RATHER ...

Be Turned To A Door That Never Closed
Or A Closed Door That Never Open?

Swim In A Pool Of Sharks Or Play
On A Field Of Cotton Candy?

Would You RATHER ...

Be Forced To Sing Each Time A Song Was On Your Mind Or To Never Talk Unless Someone Praise You?

Blow Out 100 Butterflies Every Time You Yawn Or Each Time Your Draw A Mouse Out?

Would You RATHER ...

Have Tiny Hand Of A Fairy And Huge Feet Of Giant Or Become A Dwarf?

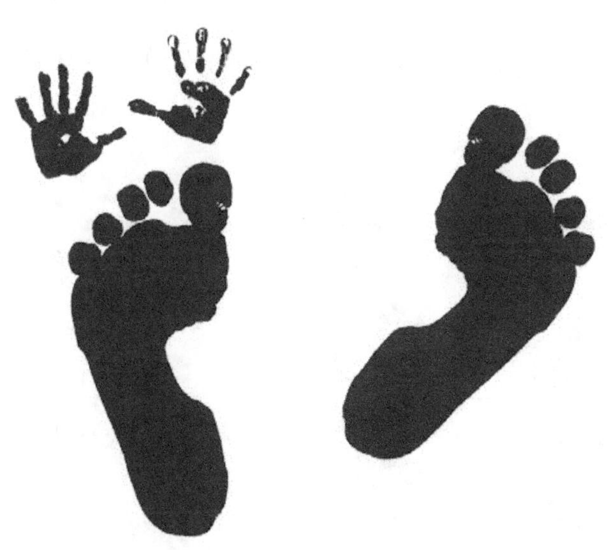

Run As Fast As A Rabbit Or Run As Fast As A Snail But Not Be Able To Fly?

Would You RATHER ...

Be Wearing Any Type Of Clothing That You Want To School Or Wearing Just School Uniform?

Go Back In Time 10 Years Or Go Into The Future 20 Years From Now?

Would You RATHER ...

Have To Wash Your Hair With Baking Soda Or Dish Soap?

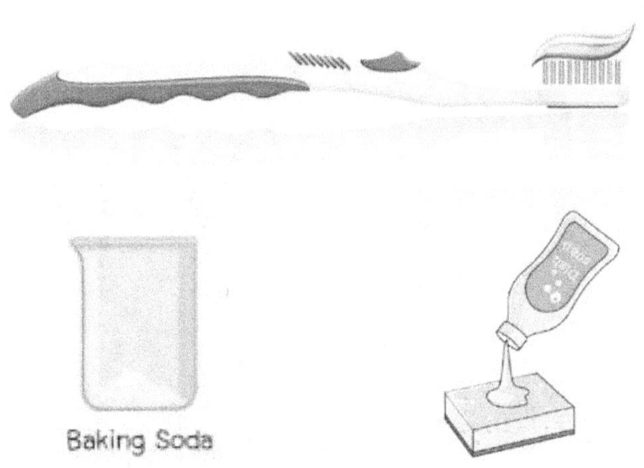

Name Your Own Pet Dog Or Be Able To Name Your Own School Bag?

Would You RATHER ...

Have A 4 Pair Of Eyes On The Back Of Your Head Or 2 Pair Of Eyes On One Side Of Your Head?

Visit A Flyer Once Every Month Or Go To A Planet That Rain Diamond Once Every Year?

Would You RATHER ...

Walk With Hands Or Write With Feet?

 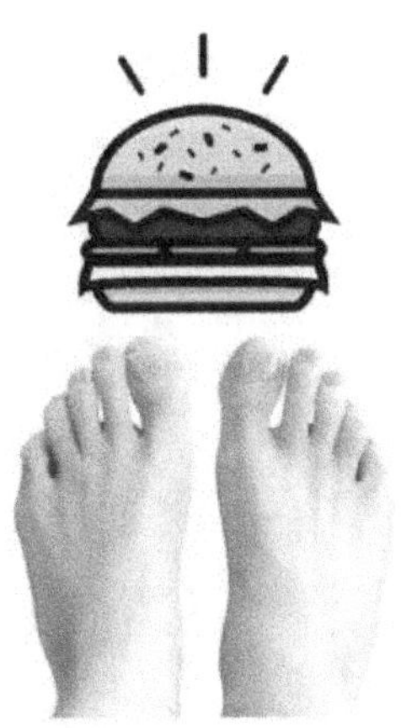

Have To Ride Bus Or Horse To School Every Day?

Would You RATHER ...

Every Shirt You Wear Be Kind Small Or Only Be Able To Use 1 Ply Of Toilet Paper?

Live On A Sunny Island Or Life In A Planet That Is Super Cold?

Would You RATHER ...

Have Spaghetti Hair As Food To Eat For Life Or Maple Syrup To Drink?

Have To Laugh Out Loud Each Time You Speak Or Cry Every Time You Read?

Would You RATHER ...

Be Insane To Eat A 20 Hamburgers
All At Once Or Drink 20 Bottles
Of Coke For A Week?

Have The Super Power To See
Things Very Small Or To See Things
Very Far?

Would You RATHER ...

Be To Control When It Rains Or When The Sun Is Out?

Lose The Ability To Read Someone Or Lose The Ability To Sing Very Well?

Would You RATHER ...

Turned Into A Monkey
Or Into A Mermaid?

Speak To Birds Or Be Able To
Speak To Dogs?

Would You RATHER ...

Always Be 10 Minutes Late Or
Always Be 20 Minutes Early?

Have A Magic Wand That Can
Turn Anything Into What You
Want Or Able To Pause Time?

Would You RATHER ...

Be An Eagle That Fly Or Turtle That Live In The Sea?

Possess The Ability To Turn Your Classmate Into Invisible Or Have Your Teacher Turned Into A Frog?

Would You RATHER ...

Have Traffic Lights That Turn
Green Whenever You Are Near
Or Never Have To Wait For Bus Again?

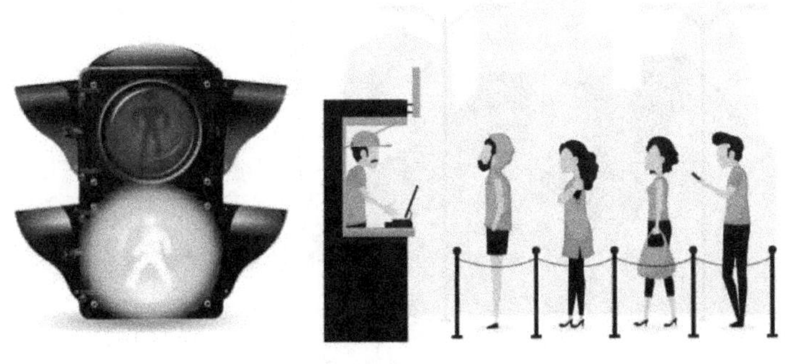

Spend The Rest Of Your Life On
The Moon As Home Or Tree House
As Home?

Would You RATHER ...

Become A Giant Pair Of Shoes
For Life Or A Tiny Baby Shoes Forever?

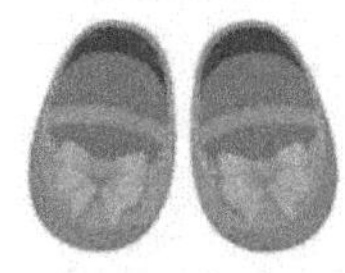

Have Eyeballs Made Of Chocolate Or
Nose Made Of Lollipop?

Would You RATHER ...

Be As Thin As A Sheet Or Paper Or
As Fat As A Giant Hot Air Balloon?

Be Able To Push Things Away
From You Or Pull Them Towards
You Just By Looking At Them?

Would You RATHER ...

Have Tree That Grow 10 Times Larger Than Normal Or Have Elephants Shrink 10 Times Smaller?

Have Your House Float On Water Or Float In The Space?

Would You RATHER ...

Have Ears That Lit Up Every
Time You Got Angry Or A Nose That
Turned Bright Red Every Time You Lie?

Have A Sister Who Doesn't Play
With You Or One Who Does Know
How To Cook Well?

Would You RATHER ...

Have To Wear A Clown Mask Or
A Superhero Mask Every Day
For The Rest Of Your Life?

Be Eating A Plate Of Scramble Eggs
With Ants Or Eating A Plate
Of Cooked Frog Legs?

Would You RATHER ...

Have A Robot As Friend
Or Have An Alien Friend
Of A Different Planet?

Have Robots Or Space Aliens
Invade Our Planet And Take Over
Our World?

Would You RATHER ...

Receive $50 Each Time You
Make Someone Laugh Or
$10 For Making Someone Cry?

Not Brush Your Teeth In The
Morning Or Not Having Breakfast
Before School?

Would You RATHER ...

Eat A Sandwich With No Bread
Or A Cheeseburger With No Cheese?

Grow Horns Like Buffalo Or Grow A
Tail Like A Monkey?

Would You RATHER ...

Have Eyebrows That Shaped Like Brid Or Have 4 Eyebrows On Your Face?

Wear A Red Canvas Shoes To School Or Slippers Everywhere You Go?

Would You RATHER ...

Be Able To Eat Like An Elephant Or Sleep As Much As You Want Everyday?

Have To Wrestle A Shark Or A Leopard?

Would You RATHER ...

Start Your Life Different Than Now Or Be Born As Animal?

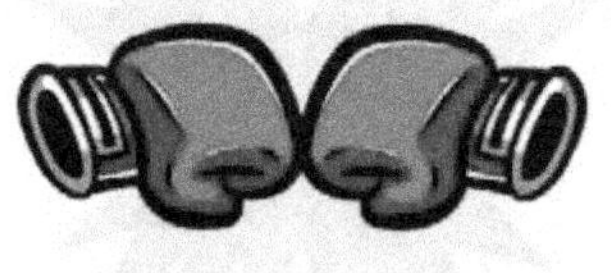

Have Hands That Were Wheels Or Have Feet That Were Boxing Gloves?

Would You RATHER ...

Have Slimy Body Like A Snake
For Teeth Or Sharp Talons
Like An Eagle As Fingers?

Drink Vegetable Juice Or Eat
Printed Meat From Vegetables?

Would You RATHER ...

Be Bald Or Have A Bad Hair Day Every Single Day?

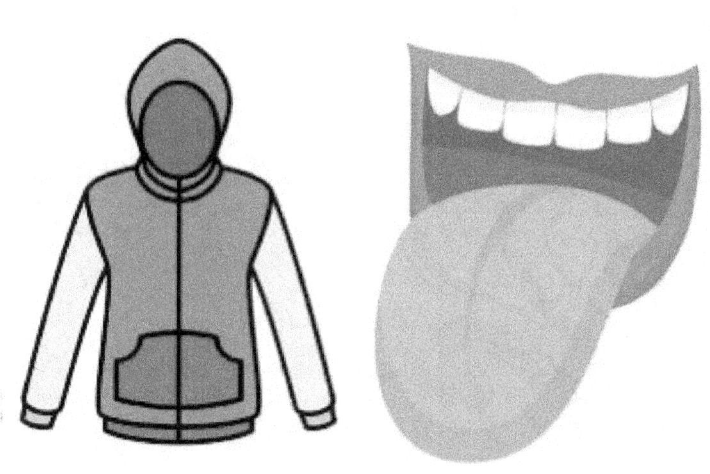

Wash Your Shoes Or Lick Your Dishes With Your Tongue?

Would You RATHER ...

Say Hello To Every Person You Saw Or Never Be Able To Say A Word To Anybody?

Wake Up In The Morning And Be By The Beach Or In Another Country?

Would You RATHER ...

Have Extremely Long Arms That Touch The Floor Or Extreme Short Legs?

Get Stuck In A House With 5 Monkeys Or With 100 People?

Would You RATHER ...

Laugh Every Time Someone Said You're Pretty Or Cry Every Time Someone Said You're Smart?

Be Able To Control When You Grow Up Or When You Can Have Ice Cream ?

Would You RATHER ...

Shrink To The Size Of A Pea Whenever You Sneezed Or Grow Into A Giant When You Coughed?

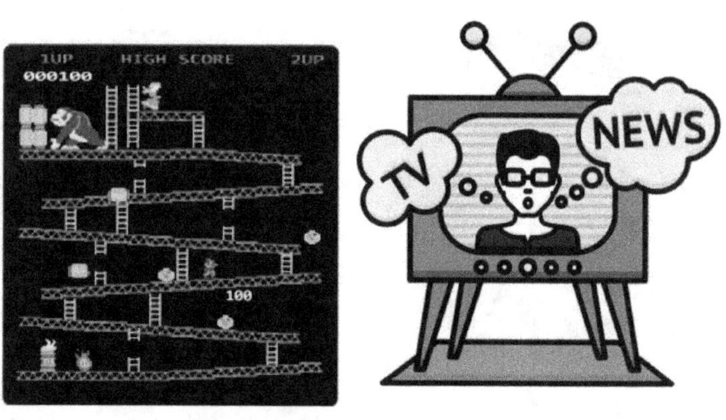

Be A Character In A Video Game Or Be a TV News Presenter?

Would You RATHER ...

Be Able To Travel The Entire
World in 80 Days Or Spend
1 Year In A Country You Love?
?

Have To Dye Your Hair Green Or
Shave Off All Your Hair?

Would You RATHER ...

Have A Dinosaurs Or The Woolly Mammoth As Pet?

Have Your Grandfather's Pocket Watch Or Have Your Grandfather's Life Journal?

Would You RATHER ...

Wear A Tuxedo Or Wear A
Swimming Trunk To School Every Day?

Have An Unlimited Amount Of
Gold Coin Or Have Unlimited
Amount of Food Every Day?

Would You RATHER ...

Have To Take Milk Bath
Or A Honey Shower Every Morning?

Be In Jail For 2 Years Or Stay On
An Island Full Of Poisonous Snake?

Would You RATHER ...

Possess The Ability To See-Through Wall Or Be Able To Talk To Animals?

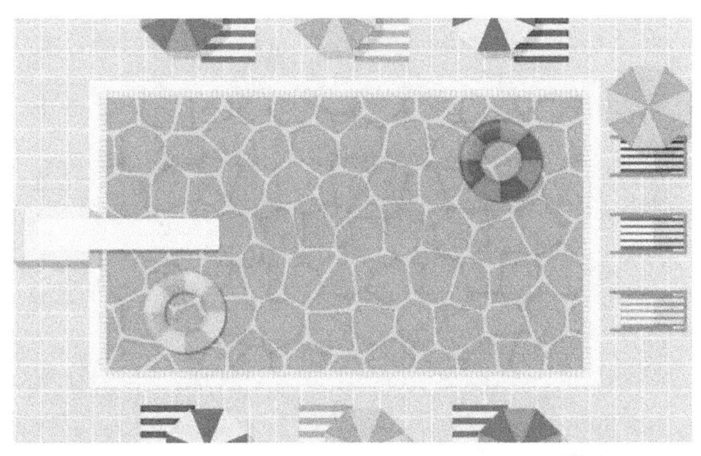

Swim In A Swimming Pool With 10 Goats Or With 100 Mice?

Would You RATHER ...

Be Able To Hear What Your Parents Think Or What Your Teacher Think?

Be An Island Or A Sea-turtle That Swim Freely?

Would You RATHER ...

Be Born As A Pig Or
Born As An Elephant?

Wear An Oversized Shirt Or Pink
Shoes To School Every Day?

Would You RATHER ...

Have Tomato Sauce All Over Your Face Or Have Chili Sauce Over Your Feet?

Sleep In BBQ Sauce Or Get Chased By Mustard Sauce In Your Dream?

Would You RATHER ...

Have An Oversized Pet Cat
Size Of A Lion Or A Tiny Lion
The Size Of Pet Cat?

Go To A Water Amusement Park
Or Play With Transparent
Inflatable Ball At The Park?

Would You RATHER ...

Be A King That Milk Cow Daily Or A Cow That Turned Into A King?

Turn The Drink You Drink Into Coffee Or Sewage Water Every Single Time?

Would You RATHER ...

Be Friend With All The Dogs In The World Or With Birds That Fly?

Be Able To Turn The Moon Into Cracker Or Your School Into California Pizza?

Would You RATHER ...

Turn Into A Puppy That Can Speak
Or Turn Into A
Cat Every Time You Fall Asleep?

Wear A Singlet During Winter Or
Super Thick Clothing During
Summer ?

Would You RATHER ...

Be The Most Popular Person In School
Or An Ordinary Person Besides A King?

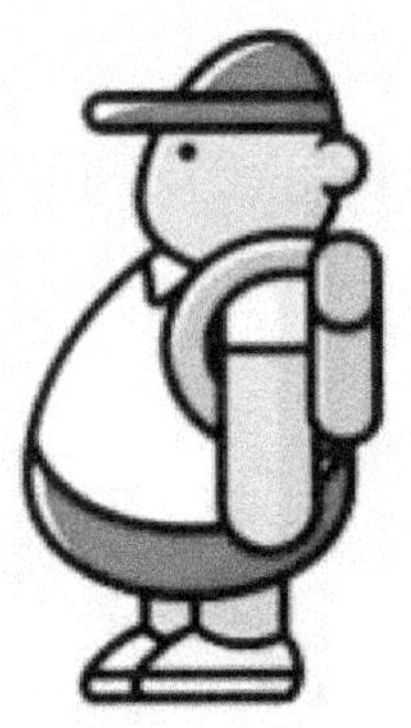

Have Skin That Like Snakes Or Fur
Like Lion All Over Your Body?

Would You RATHER ...

Live In The Hottest Desert
Or In The Deepest Ocean ?

Be An Alien With Two Heads And
Super Smart or A Giraffe That Could
Speak French?

Would You RATHER ...

Smell Like A Rubbish Dump But Rich
Or Have Bad Breath But Smart?

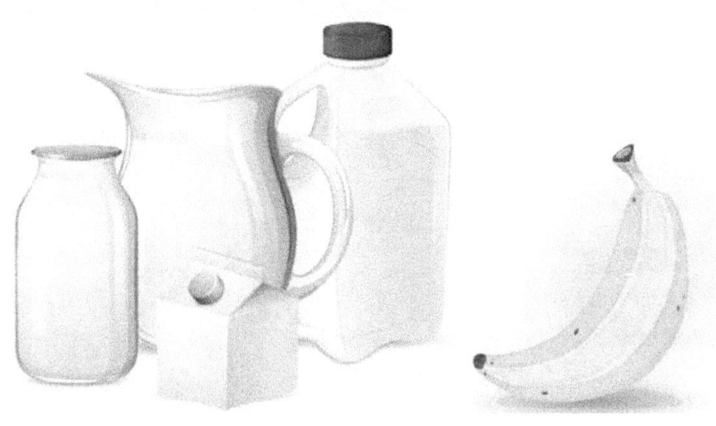

Have To Drink Milk For Life Or Eat
Banana For As Long As You Lived?

Would You RATHER ...

Be Eaten By A 30-foot Anaconda Or Crushed Over By An Elephant?

Have To Poop 100 Times Every Day Or Step On Dog Poop Every Day When You Walk Outside Your House?

Would You RATHER ...

Have To Eat Burned Food Or
Rotten Apples Every Day?

Have To Eat Frog's Legs Or Pig's
Feet Every Meal For The Rest Of
Your Life?

Would You RATHER ...

Every Day Having Your Favorite Drink Or Eating Maggots For Every Meal?

Have To Use Leaves For Your Toilet Paper Or Mayonnaise For Your Soap?

Would You RATHER ...

Have To Wear A Stinky Pair Of Shoes Or Socks To School Every Day?

Have To Smell Your Own Sweaty Armpit Or Smell Someone Else Smelly Socks Every Day?

Would You RATHER ...

Have To Eat Slimy Sardines Or
Cow Liver For Every Meal
The Rest Of Your Life?

Have A Baby Cry Or Poop On You
Each Time You Carry Him?

Would You RATHER ...

Not Wash Your Underwear Or Not Clean Your Table For An Entire Week?

Step On Dog Poop Or Poison Ivy While Walking Outside?

Would You RATHER ...

Swallow Hot Chili Or
Bitter Melon For Your
All Your Meals?

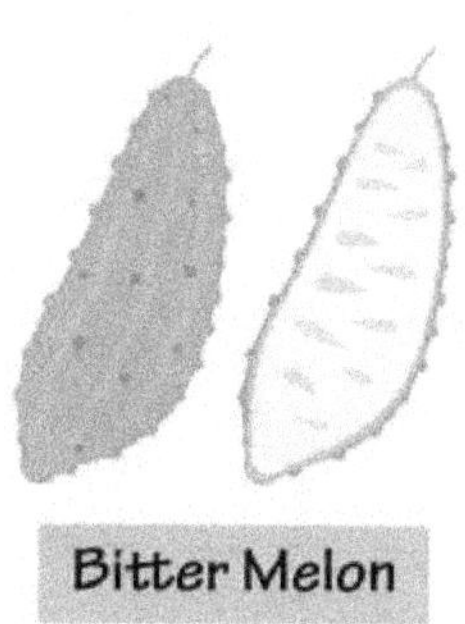

Drive A Sport Car With Big
Wheels Or A School Bus With
Small Wheels?

Would You RATHER ...

Possess The Ability To Buy Anything You Like Or The Ability To Stop Time?

Have 100 Aggressive Wasps Chasing You Or 10 Super Stinky Skunks In Your Bedroom?

Would You RATHER ...

Have A Running Nose Or Blocked Nose For A School Day?

Ask A Giant For Direction Or A Gangster From The Street

Would You RATHER ...

Play With Pigs In Mud Or Get Drenched In The Rain?

Have A Big Ears Or Big Nostrils ?

Would You RATHER ...

Be Fully Covered In Honey Or Completely Covered In Dirty Mud?

Have Ants Crawling Or Cockroaches Crawling All Over Your Body?

Would You RATHER ...

Have To Eat The Diet Of A Bear Or The Diet Of Elephant For Every Meal?

Be Unable To Wash Any Of Your Socks Or Any Of Your Shorts For The Whole Year?

Would You RATHER ...

Turn Into Your Mom Or Your Dad
For One Day If You Could
Only Choose One?

Burp In Front Of Your Teacher Or
Fart Silently In A Lift?

Would You RATHER ...

Have Hair So Long That It Touched The Ground Or Have No Hair At All For The Rest Of Your Life?

Have To Rain Honey Or Rain Sticky Syrup During Rainy Day?

Would You RATHER ...

Become A Toilet Roll Or
Become A Broom For A Day?

Use A Litter Box As Bathroom Or
Use The Bathroom Outdoors?

Would You RATHER ...

Have To Yawn Every 10 Minutes Or Burp Every 10 Minutes?

Pet A Lion Or Pet A Panda For 10 Minutes?

Would You RATHER ...

Have To Fried Wasp
Or A Fried Earth Worm?

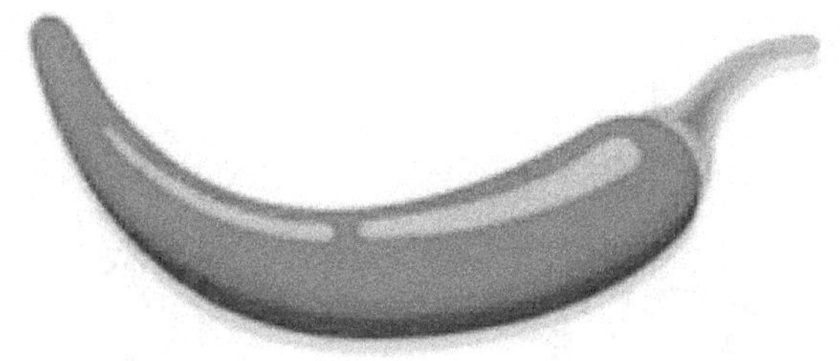

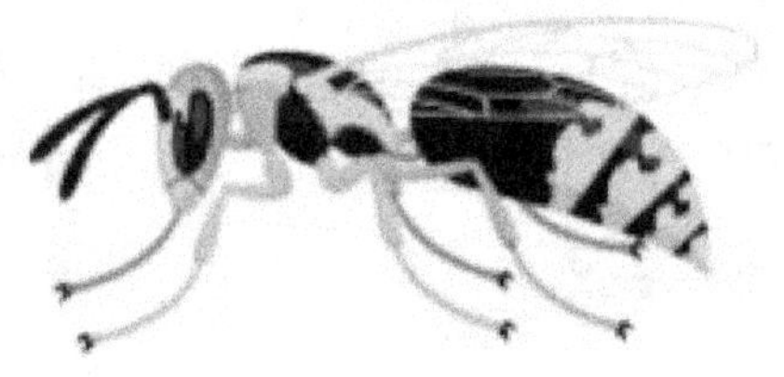

Be Heard Every Time You Burp Or
Every Time You Fart?

Would You RATHER ...

Eat 10 Hot Dog In 30 Minutes
Or 100 Cheeseburger In 30 Days?

Have To Smell A Rotten Egg Every
Morning Or Go To The Garbage
Dump Every Afternoon?

Would You RATHER ...

Have Pooped Your Pants Every Time
You Stand Up Or Pee
Each Time You Sing?

Have To Lick A Trashcan Or Eat
Moldy Fish As Food?

Would You RATHER ...

Eat A Bunch Of Bitter Grape
Or Drinks Water From
The Smelly Drain?

Have Gum Stuck On Your Pants Or
In Between Your Book Pages?

Would You RATHER ...

Sweat Every Single Time You Pee Or Take Shower Once A Month?

Have 100 Crocodiles In Your Room Or Have To Eat One Cockroach Alive?

Would You RATHER ...

Not Be Able To Brush Your Teeth
Again Or Have To Shower
10 Times Everyday?

Forget To Bring Your Textbook Or
Forget To Bring Your Pencil
Case To School?

Would You RATHER ...

Have A Green Salad Or Eat Oysters For Breakfast?

Dress In Pink Neon Or Black For The Rest Of Your Life?

Would You RATHER ...

Wear Paper Socks And Underwear
Or A Used Toothbrush?

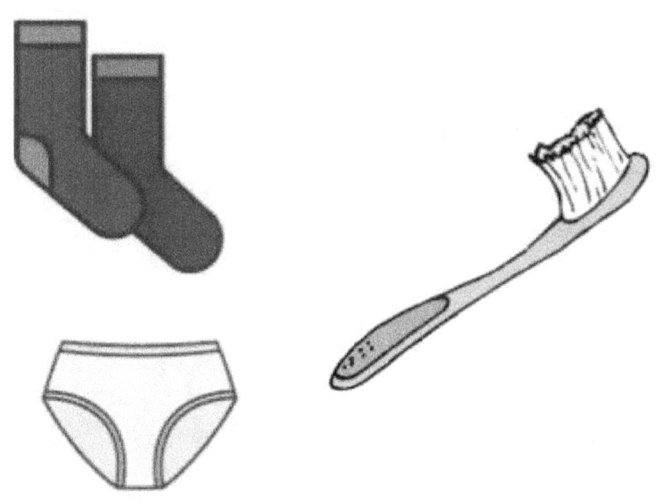

Have To Smell Your Worn Clothing Or
Your Socks Every Morning?

Would You RATHER ...

Poop Lemon Or Pee Green Tea Every
Time You Go To The Bathroom?

Learn How To Swim Or Dive In
The Smelliest Drain?

Would You RATHER ...

Pee Outside The Toilet Bowl Or Poop Outside The Toilet Bowl?

Drink Red Colored Water Or Blue Colored Water But Not Knowing What It Is?

Would You RATHER ...

Have 3 Arms
Or 6 Feet ?

Drink Mug Water With Bugs Or
Drink Slime Made From A Snail?

Would You RATHER ...

Let Someone Cut Your Toenails or Have Your Toenails Pulled Out?

Come Across A Rat Running Under Your Feet Or Have Milk And Cornflakes All Over Your Body?

Would You RATHER ...

Be Able To Swimming Faster Than Sharks Or Be Eaten Alive By Sharks?

Wash Your Friend's Smelly Feet Or Have Your Friend Wash Your Smelly Feet?

REMEMBER
Claim Your FREE Printable Colored Bookmarks From

https://rebrand.ly/freebookmarks

"IF YOU LIKE THIS BOOK, DO LEAVE US A REVIEW. THANK YOU!"